Rookie
Read-About®
Safety

Internet
Safety

by Lisa M. Herrington

Content Consultant
Debra Holtzman, J.D., M.A.

Reading Consultant
Jeanne Clidas, Ph.D.
Reading Specialist

Children's Press®
An Imprint of Scholastic Inc.
New York Toronto London Auckland Sydney
Mexico City New Delhi Hong Kong
Danbury, Connecticut

Dear Parent/Educator:
It is very important that children learn how to be safe online.
However, this is something they might need help with from
a grown-up. If your child needs that help, we hope you will
use this book as a springboard to a discussion about Internet
safety with him or her. You can read the book together the
first time, and talk about the different suggestions inside.

Library of Congress Cataloging-in-Publication Data
Herrington, Lisa M.
   Internet safety / by Lisa M. Herrington.
      p. cm.— (Rookie read-about safety)
   Includes index.
   ISBN 978-0-531-28971-6 (library binding)   ISBN 978-0-531-29273-0 (pbk.)
1. Internet and children—Juvenile literature. 2. Internet—Safety measures—
Juvenile literature. 3. Safety education—Juvenile literature. I. Title.
HQ784.I58H45 2013
004.67'8083—dc23   2012013376

Produced by Spooky Cheetah Press

Photographs © 2013: Alamy Images/AJSlife: 16; Getty Images/Alexandra
Grablewski: cover; Shutterstock, Inc./Dmitriy Shironosov: 4; Thinkstock: 11
(Ableimages), 8 (BananaStock), 3 bottom (Fuse), 19 (Hemera), 3 top, 12, 15, 23, 27,
28, 31 top right, 31 bottom left, 31 bottom right (iStockphoto), 20, 24 (Jupiterimages/
Getty Images), 7 (Pixland), 31 top left (Ryan McVay).

Table of Contents

What Is the Internet?

Some kids play games
on the computer.
Some of the games
are online.

To go online means you are using the Internet. The Internet connects computers around the world.

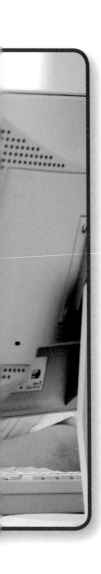

You can find facts and play games by going online. But being safe is important.

Online Smarts

Be sure to go online with a grown-up. Only visit Web sites an adult says you can.

Do not believe everything you see online. Some people may post things that are wrong.

Think Before You Click

When you are online, you may see a box pop up. Do not click on any box or question that you see.

Some people go online to talk to people they know or to connect to new people.

You should not talk to anyone you do not know online. Do not tell a stranger your name or anything about yourself.

Stay Away from Strangers!

If someone you do not know tries to talk to you online, do not talk to the person. Tell a grown-up.

Computer Rules

If you are online with a friend, remember the rules. Do not let anyone push you to break them.

Follow your family's computer rules. Do your homework before you use the computer.

Do not sit in front of the computer too long. Get off when your time is up. Go outside and play!

The Internet can be fun as long as you use online smarts!

Try It! Read the tip on page 10 again. Ask a grown-up to help you find web sites that are okay to visit.

I Can Be Safe!

- Only visit Web sites an adult you trust says you can.

- Tell a grown-up if someone is mean to you online.

- Do not talk to strangers online.

- Never give out your personal information.

- Do not sit in front of the computer too long.

Words You Know

computer

kids

people

play

Index

Facts for Now

Visit this Scholastic Web site for more information on Internet safety:
www.factsfornow.scholastic.com
Enter the keyword **Internet**

About the Author

Lisa M. Herrington writes print and digital materials for kids, teachers, and parents. She lives in Connecticut with her husband and daughter. She hopes all kids stay safe!